D0608843

The Great Jewish cartoon book

The Great Jewish cartoon book

Neil Kerber

Robson Books

First published in Great Britain in 1996 by
Robson Books, 10 Blenheim Court, Brewery
Road, London N7 9NT
Reprinted 1996, 2000

Copyright © 1996 Neil Kerber
The right of Neil Kerber to be identified as
author of this work har been asserted by him
in accordance with the Copyright, Designs
and Patents Act 1988

**British Library Cataloguing in Pub-
lication Data**
A catalogue record for this title is available
from the British Library

ISBN 1 86105 023 2

All rights reserved. No part of this
publication may be reproduced, stored in a
retrieval system, or transmitted in any form
or by any means, electronic, mechanical,
photocopying, recording or otherwise,
without the prior permission in writing of the
publishers.

Printed in Finland by WS Bookwell Ltd

To my parents, aka Evelyn and Bernie,
who made me a Jew . . . and are therefore responsible
for any traumas caused by this book.

Foreword

When approached to compile this book I decided
that I would need to delve into my soul in order to
create the true comic spirit of the Jewish race.

Then I thought, 'what the heck?' and just drew a
load of cartoons . . .

Jewish Man:

Jewish Martial Arts.....

'... *First you must learn to chop a liver* ...'

'I can do you a nice chop ... and also maybe some meat for dinner?'

'Don't worry, Bernie, they're harmless ... they keep themselves
to themselves.'

THE INVISIBLE MAN
(YIDDISHE VERSION)

'I'm looking for Long John Silverman ...'

ROMEO AND JULI-YENTA

According to ancient Jewish legend, Oedipus Kleinman,
unaware of his own identity, killed his father and fell in love
with his mother's cooking.

The Jewish Princess and the frog.

'Honey, did you you remember to put the Katz out?'

'And tomorrow we'll be asking, "Does your man prefer someone else's soup?"'

How Picasso got started:

'I like your style, Pablo, but maybe you should think about branching out and not just doing bar mitzvah portraits.'

'... And do you, Emma Louise Hershenblum, take Irving Saul's credit card, to have and to spend on dresses and facial saunas, so long as you both shall live?'

Jewish cannibals.

'Right, Batman, you round up all evil. Superman, you save
the world. And Goldman – you get the bagels.'

'Apparently it's all blood and guts.'

'There's something weird about your work, Henry ... and it
seems to be ever since you started eating those "bagel"
things ...'

'I'm not sure about this new wailing wallpaper, Harry ...'

Jewish grandma
horticulturalists.

'Bad hair day!'

Jewrobics.

'Well, you're not pregnant, Mrs Broomstein, but I'm sending
you down to the excessive noshing ward for some tests.'

IF I WERE A RICH MAN........

'All those in favour say "Oy".'

'I wouldn't say my mother-in-law's fatty ...'

Isaac Newton discovers Judaism.....

'Son, it's time you knew ... we're not your real parents.'

'Excuse me, sir ... Have you thought about head cover?'

'OK, when I give the signal I want you to have a ten-minute argument with me about who's supposed to be navigating...'

'It's an accountant!!'

Although hardly ever mentioned in history books, it is now known that the Jewish Vikings were particularly savage in the eighth century, taking business cards and stealing clients from whichever country they invaded.

'Calm down, honey! Why do you always get like this when
Barry Manilow's on the radio?!'

BERGMAN OF ALCATRAZ.

Farmer Abraham Schwartz and his famous schmuckspreader.

Door-to-door Jewish parent.

'So that's the food and the band sorted. Now let's have a flick through Renta Yenta.'

'Wow, what a coincidence! We both don't eat pork...'

Pearl diving in Florida.

Early Jews.

If I were a rich man...

'Irving's parents wanted Jewish grandchildren, so I
converted...'

'I know, I know ... but when I said "take me to your leader" I didn't think it would be such a schlap!'

'Erm ... we've decided not to have the kid circumcised, Rabbi
Shakeman.'

Jewish Mafia threats.

'No, Miss, the Ladies is down the corridor...'

New York 1903. Irwin Bagel makes an important suggestion.

'Sarah, could you send in two teas, please? Oh, and some biscuits. And a small selection of pastries ... Maybe some parcels of salmon in filo pastry, served with a wild mushroom sauce and a dash of asparagus mousse ...'

'Great. Of all the tribes we could've come across, we had to
run in to the Meshuggenas!'

Meanwhile, at Jewish Auntie school...

70s Hassidics.

Young Steven Spielberg.

'Good morning, Mr Shylock. Your usual pound of flesh?'

'So, comrades, it's all agreed then ... Tomorrow we get rid of farmer Cohen. I'll talk to my brother Irwin, the accountant, who'll draw up the papers!'

'I decided to go for many colours this Autumn. I haven't actually done that with dreamcoats before, but hopefully it should get a lot of publicity.'

Old Jewish proverb say:
    'If a tree falls in a forest and there
    is no one around to hear it,
    Why should I get involved? Trees are not my thing.
    What does a Jew know about trees?'

Woolly Allen.

If I were a rich man....

Trouble at the OK, already, My life:

'You got a broygus with me, Ernie?'

'Careful, darling, he might have rabbies.'

'Harvey! It's me! I need some money to buy a dress for the Kershman's wedding ...'

Arranged marriage:

Very Arranged marriage:

The Jazz Singer's father on holiday.

THE BRADY MACCABI BUNCH

'It's a blessing in disguise.'

The National Auntie Lottie.

JEWISH WEIGHT WATCHERS

'In the event of an emergency your life jacket can be found under your seat. It's the inflatable orange thing – although we do have it in a nice key-lime green, similar to the colour that Barbara Nershberg wore at the Glookman wedding.'

'Look, Harry, Miami!!'